THE MUFFINS ARE COMING

BY THERESA NELL MILLANG

This cookbook is designed to keep as a whole book, or to mail separate recipes by simply tearing out the desired perforated gift recipe card, and address on the back side.

WALDMAN HOUSE PRESS
Minneapolis, Minnesota

Waldman House Press
525 North Third Street
Minneapolis, Minnesota 55401

ISBN: 0-931674-15-8
Printed in the USA

A WORD ABOUT INGREDIENTS

OAT BRAN. That's what you've been hearing about... how important oat bran is for your diet. Oat bran has been proven to help reduce cholesterol levels significantly.

PLEASE NOTE...

All muffins in this collection of recipes are made without using egg yolk—reducing cholesterol intake. Egg yolk has the highest cholesterol count of any food item. As a general comparison: 1 egg yolk contains 275 milligrams of cholesterol, 1 cup of whole milk 33 milligrams, and 1 pound of hamburger 295 milligrams.

The American Heart Association recommends that intake of cholesterol be limited, and not to exceed 300 milligrams per day.

CONTENTS

Theresa Millang published her first cookbook,
Roux Roux Roux, a comprehensive Cajun cookbook,
in 1986. Theresa lives in Minneapolis, Minnesota.

APPLE

Makes 12 Muffins

DRY INGREDIENTS

1¼ Cups oat bran
1¼ Cups all-purpose flour
3 Tsp baking powder
½ Cup brown sugar
½ Tsp salt
1 Tsp cinnamon
2 Tsp non-fat dry milk
¼ Cup chopped walnuts

WET INGREDIENTS

¾ Cup skim milk
1 Tbs lemon juice
3 Egg whites, beaten with
  2 tsp corn oil
¼ Cup corn oil
1 Tsp vanilla
¼ Cup raisins
2 Cups chopped apples

Preheat oven to 400°F
Grease or paper line muffin pan.

---

1 *In large bowl, combine all the dry ingredients. Mix well.*
2 *In medium bowl, combine all wet ingredients. Mix well.*
3 *Combine dry and wet ingredients. Stir only to moisten, but batter is lumpy. Spoon into muffin pan and bake 20 to 25 minutes. Remove from pan and cool on rack.*

THIS HARDY MUFFIN IS CHOCK-FULL OF NUTS AND RAISINS. SERVE WITH CINNAMON HONEY!

A *CARD-GIFT* Recipe

OAT BRAN *Muffin*

To:

PUMPKIN

Makes 12 Muffins

DRY INGREDIENTS

⅔ Cup oat bran
1¼ Cups all-purpose flour
2 Tsp baking powder
½ Cup sugar
¼ Tsp cinnamon
¼ Tsp nutmeg
½ Tsp salt
1 Tsp non-fat dry milk
½ Cup chopped pecans

WET INGREDIENTS

¾ Cup skim milk
1 Tsp vanilla
2 Egg whites, beaten with
1 tsp corn oil
¼ Cup margarine, melted
½ Cup raisins
½ Cup cooked pumpkin

Preheat oven to 400°F
Grease or paper line muffin pan.

1 *In large bowl, combine all the dry ingredients. Mix well.*
2 *In medium bowl, combine all wet ingredients. Mix well.*
3 *Combine dry and wet ingredients. Stir only to moisten, but batter is lumpy. Spoon into muffin pan and bake 20 to 25 minutes. Remove from pan and cool on rack.*

SERVE THESE ON SPECIAL HOLIDAYS FOR A LIGHT EVENING SNACK.

A *CARD-GIFT* Recipe

OAT BRAN *Muffin*

To:

FRESH PEACH

Makes 12 Muffins

DRY INGREDIENTS

1 Cup oat bran
1¼ Cups all-purpose flour
2½ Tsp baking powder
½ Tsp salt
½ Cup sugar
½ Tsp cinnamon
¼ Tsp nutmeg
1 Tsp non-fat dry milk

WET INGREDIENTS

¾ Cup skim milk
2 Egg whites, beaten with
  1 tsp corn oil
¼ Cup margarine, melted
1 Tbs fresh lemon juice
1 Tsp grated lemon rind
1 Cup fresh peaches, peeled
  and cut into chunks
1 Tsp vanilla

Preheat oven to 400°F
Grease or paper line muffin pan.

1 In large bowl, combine all the dry ingredients. Mix well.
2 In medium bowl, combine all wet ingredients. Mix well.
3 Combine dry and wet ingredients. Stir only to moisten, but batter is lumpy. Spoon into muffin pan and bake 20 to 25 minutes. Remove from pan and cool on rack.

THE DELICATE PEACH FLAVOR IS ENHANCED WITH SPICES. USE CANNED WHEN FRESH NOT AVAILABLE.

A *CARD-GIFT* Recipe

OAT BRAN *Muffin*

To:

PEANUT BUTTER

Makes 12 Muffins

DRY INGREDIENTS

1 Cup oat bran
1 Cup all-purpose flour
2 Tsp baking powder
¼ Tsp baking soda
½ Tsp salt
½ Cup brown sugar
1 Tsp non-fat dry milk

WET INGREDIENTS

1 Cup skim milk
½ Cup peanut butter, chunky
2 Tbs margarine, melted
2 Egg whites, beaten with 1 tsp corn oil
1 Tsp vanilla

Preheat oven to 400°F
Grease or paper line muffin pan.

---

1 *In large bowl, combine all the dry ingredients. Mix well.*
2 *In medium bowl, combine all wet ingredients. Mix well.*
3 *Combine dry and wet ingredients. Stir only to moisten, but batter is lumpy. Spoon into muffin pan and bake 20 to 25 minutes. Remove from pan and cool on rack.*

ROUND UP THE GANG FOR THIS NUTRITIOUS MUFFIN. BE SURE TO HAVE PLENTY ON HAND!

A *CARD-GIFT* Recipe

OAT BRAN *Muffin*

To:

FRESH STRAWBERRY

Makes 12 Muffins

DRY INGREDIENTS

1 Cup oat bran
1¼ Cups all-purpose flour
½ Cup sugar
2 Tsp baking powder
½ Tsp salt
2 Tsp non-fat dry milk

WET INGREDIENTS

⅔ Cup skim milk
3 Egg whites, beaten with
  1 tsp corn oil
¼ Cup margarine, melted
1 Tsp vanilla
1 Tsp lemon juice
2 Cups strawberries, cut
  into small pieces

Preheat oven to 400°F
Grease or paper line muffin pan.

---

1 *In large bowl, combine all the dry ingredients. Mix well.*
2 *In medium bowl, combine all wet ingredients. Mix well.*
3 *Combine dry and wet ingredients. Stir only to moisten, but batter is lumpy. Spoon into muffin pan and bake 20 to 25 minutes. Remove from pan and cool on rack.*

PICK THE FIRM BERRIES FOR BEST RESULTS WHEN BAKING THESE SPECIAL MUFFINS.

A *CARD-GIFT* Recipe

OAT BRAN *Muffin*

To:

CARROT

Makes 12 Muffins
DRY INGREDIENTS

⅔ Cup oat bran
⅔ Cup whole wheat flour
⅔ Cup all-purpose flour
½ Cup brown sugar
2½ Tsp baking powder
½ Tsp salt
1 Tsp cinnamon, scant
2 Tsp non-fat dry milk
½ Cup chopped walnuts

WET INGREDIENTS

2 Egg whites, beaten with
  2 tsp corn oil
⅔ Cup skim milk
½ Cup coconut flakes
1 Cup shredded carrots
1 Tsp vanilla
¼ Cup corn oil

Preheat oven to 400°F
Grease or paper line muffin pan.

1 *In large bowl, combine all the dry ingredients. Mix well.*
2 *In medium bowl, combine all wet ingredients. Mix well.*
3 *Combine dry and wet ingredients. Stir only to moisten, but batter is lumpy. Spoon into muffin pan and bake 20 to 25 minutes. Remove from pan and cool on rack.*

THIS RECIPE MAKES A MOIST SPICY MUFFIN. SERVE THESE WITH A FRESH FRUIT SALAD.

A *CARD-GIFT* Recipe

OAT BRAN *Muffin*

To:

BLACKBERRY
Makes 12 Muffins

DRY INGREDIENTS

1 Cup oat bran
1¼ Cups all-purpose flour
2½ Tsp baking powder
½ Tsp salt
½ Cup sugar
2 Tsp non-fat dry milk

WET INGREDIENTS

2 Egg whites, beaten with
  1 tsp corn oil
¾ Cup skim milk
¼ Cup margarine, melted
1 Tsp vanilla
1 Cup fresh blackberries

Preheat oven to 400°F
Grease or paper line muffin pan.

---

1 In large bowl, combine all the dry ingredients. Mix well.
2 In medium bowl, combine all wet ingredients. Mix well.
3 Combine dry and wet ingredients. Stir only to moisten, but batter is lumpy. Spoon into muffin pan and bake 20 to 25 minutes. Remove from pan and cool on rack.

CAPTURE THE DEW FRESH FLAVOR OF BLACKBERRIES IN THIS TASTY MUFFIN. SERVE WARM.

A *CARD-GIFT* Recipe

OAT BRAN *Muffin*

To:

BANANA
Makes 12 Muffins

DRY INGREDIENTS

1½ Cups oat bran
1 Cup all-purpose flour
½ Cup sugar
3 Tsp baking powder
½ Tsp salt
1 Tsp non-fat dry milk
½ Cup chopped walnuts

WET INGREDIENTS

2 Egg whites, beaten with
  1 tsp corn oil
1 Cup skim milk
1 Tbs fresh lemon juice
¼ Cup corn oil
1 Tsp vanilla
2 Ripe bananas, mashed

Preheat oven to 400°F
Grease or paper line muffin pan.

---

1 *In large bowl, combine all the dry ingredients. Mix well.*
2 *In medium bowl, combine all wet ingredients. Mix well.*
3 *Combine dry and wet ingredients. Stir only to moisten, but batter is lumpy. Spoon into muffin pan and bake 20 to 25 minutes. Remove from pan and cool on rack.*

OFFER THIS MUFFIN WARM OR COLD. ALWAYS A HIT WITH THE KIDS!

A *CARD-GIFT* Recipe

OAT BRAN *Muffin*

To:

APPLESAUCE
Makes 12 Muffins

DRY INGREDIENTS

⅔ Cup oat bran
⅔ Cup all-purpose flour
⅔ Cup whole wheat flour
3 Tsp baking powder
½ Tsp salt
½ Tsp cinnamon
¼ Tsp nutmeg
½ Cup brown sugar
2 Tsp non-fat dry milk
⅓ Cup chopped nuts

WET INGREDIENTS

2 Egg whites, beaten with
  1 tsp corn oil
¼ Cup margarine, melted
½ Cup skim milk
1 Tsp vanilla
⅓ Cup raisins
1 Cup applesauce

Preheat oven to 400°F
Grease or paper line muffin pan.

1 In large bowl, combine all the dry ingredients. Mix well.
2 In medium bowl, combine all wet ingredients. Mix well.
3 Combine dry and wet ingredients. Stir only to moisten, but batter is lumpy. Spoon into muffin pan and bake 20 to 25 minutes. Remove from pan and cool on rack.

THIS IS A WONDERFUL MUFFIN. SERVE IT FOR AN AFTERNOON SNACK.

A *CARD-GIFT* Recipe
OAT BRAN *Muffin*

To:

OAT 'n WHEAT BRAN

Makes 12 Muffins

DRY INGREDIENTS

- ⅔ Cup oat bran
- ⅔ Cup all-purpose flour
- ½ Cup brown sugar
- 2 Tsp baking powder
- ½ Tsp baking soda
- 1 Tsp non-fat dry milk
- ⅓ Cup chopped walnuts

WET INGREDIENTS

- 2 Egg whites, beaten with
  1 tsp corn oil
- ¼ Cup corn oil
- 1 Tsp vanilla
- ⅓ Cup raisins
- 1 Cup all-bran, soaked in
  1 cup skim milk 3 minutes

Preheat oven to 400° F
Grease or paper line muffin pan.

1 *In large bowl, combine all the dry ingredients. Mix well.*
2 *In medium bowl, combine all wet ingredients. Mix well.*
3 *Combine dry and wet ingredients. Stir only to moisten, but batter is lumpy. Spoon into muffin pan and bake 15 to 20 minutes. Remove from pan and cool on rack.*

BOTH BRANS ARE IMPORTANT IN YOUR DIET—EACH PROVIDE DIFFERENT BENEFITS. SERVE THESE OFTEN.

A *CARD-GIFT* Recipe

OAT BRAN *Muffin*

To:

RHUBARB
Makes 12 Muffins

DRY INGREDIENTS
⅔ Cup oat bran
1¼ Cups all-purpose flour
½ Tsp baking soda
2 Tsp baking powder
½ Tsp salt
¾ Cup brown sugar
½ Tsp cinnamon
1 Tsp non-fat dry milk
½ Cup nuts, chopped

WET INGREDIENTS
2 Egg whites, beaten with
   1 tsp corn oil
½ Cup buttermilk
⅓ Cup corn oil
1 Cup fresh or frozen
   rhubarb, cut fine
1 Tsp vanilla

*Preheat oven to 325° F
Grease or paper line muffin pan.*

Grease or paper line muffin pan.
1 *In large bowl, combine all the dry
   ingredients. Mix well.*
2 *In medium bowl, combine all wet
   ingredients. Mix well.*
3 *Combine dry and wet ingredients.
   Stir only to moisten, but batter is
   lumpy. Spoon into muffin pan and
   bake 25 to 30 minutes. Remove
   from pan and cool on rack.*

LIKE A SPRING TONIC! SERVE THESE WITH HONEY OR
STRAWBERRY JAM.

A *CARD-GIFT* Recipe

OAT BRAN *Muffin*

To:

HONEY CORN
Makes 12 Muffins

DRY INGREDIENTS

1 Cup oat bran
½ Cup corn meal
⅔ Cup all-purpose flour
2½ Tsp baking powder
½ Tsp salt
2 Tsp non-fat dry milk
¼ Cup chopped walnuts,
  or pecans

WET INGREDIENTS

3 Egg whites, beaten with
  2 tsp corn oil
2 Tbs corn oil
¾ Cup skim milk
⅓ Cup honey
1 Tsp vanilla
¼ Cup raisins
1 Cup fresh cranberries,
  halved

Preheat oven to 400° F
Grease or paper line muffin pan.

*1 In large bowl, combine all the dry
 ingredients. Mix well.*
*2 In medium bowl, combine all wet
 ingredients. Mix well.*
*3 Combine dry and wet ingredients.
 Stir only to moisten, but batter is
 lumpy. Spoon into muffin pan and
 bake 20 to 25 minutes. Remove
 from pan and cool on rack.*

THE GOODNESS OF CORN COMBINES WITH OAT BRAN
FOR A TREAT. SERVE WARM WITH MARMALADE.

A *CARD-GIFT* Recipe

OAT BRAN *Muffin*

To:

DILL 'N THYME

Makes 12 Muffins

DRY INGREDIENTS

⅔ Cup oat bran
⅔ Cup whole wheat flour
⅔ Cup all-purpose flour
3 Tsp baking powder
½ Tsp salt
1½ Tsp dried dill weed
½ Tsp dried thyme
¼ Tsp garlic powder
1 Tsp non-fat dry milk

WET INGREDIENTS

⅔ Cup skim milk
½ Cup cottage cheese
¼ Cup margarine, melted
2 Egg whites, beaten with
   1 tsp corn oil

Preheat oven to 400°F
Grease or paper line muffin pan.

---

1 *In large bowl, combine all the dry ingredients. Mix well.*
2 *In medium bowl, combine all wet ingredients. Mix well.*
3 *Combine dry and wet ingredients. Stir only to moisten, but batter is lumpy. Spoon into muffin pan and bake 20 to 25 minutes. Remove from pan and cool on rack.*

A BOWL OF SOUP BECOMES A SPECIAL MEAL WHEN YOU SERVE THESE DELICIOUS HERBED MUFFINS.

A *CARD-GIFT* Recipe

OAT BRAN *Muffin*

To:

FRESH BLUEBERRY

Makes 12 Muffins

DRY INGREDIENTS

1 Cup oat bran
1¼ Cups all-purpose flour
½ Cup sugar
3 Tsp baking powder
¾ Tsp salt
1 Tsp non-fat dry milk

WET INGREDIENTS

¾ Cup skim milk
1 Tsp vanilla
2 Egg whites, beaten with
  1 tsp corn oil
¼ Cup margarine, melted
1 Cup fresh blueberries

Preheat oven to 400°F
Grease or paper line muffin pan.

---

1 *In large bowl, combine all the dry ingredients. Mix well.*
2 *In medium bowl, combine all wet ingredients. Mix well.*
3 *Combine dry and wet ingredients. Stir only to moisten, but batter is lumpy. Spoon into muffin pan and bake 20 to 25 minutes. Remove from pan and cool on rack.*

ALWAYS A FAVORITE— WHEN THE SEASON CLAIMS THE FRESH BLUEBERRIES, TRY THE FROZEN, USING ¾ CUP.

A *CARD-GIFT* Recipe

OAT BRAN *Muffin*

To:

PINEAPPLE NUT

Makes 12 Muffins

DRY INGREDIENTS

1¼ Cups oat bran
1 Cup all-purpose flour
½ Cup sugar
2½ Tsp baking powder
½ Tsp salt
½ Cup chopped almonds
1 Tsp non-fat dry milk

WET INGREDIENTS

¼ Cup margarine, melted
1 Tsp vanilla
1 8oz can pineapple chunks,
   chopped and drained
½ Cup pineapple juice
¼ Cup skim milk
1 Apple, peeled
   and chopped
2 Egg whites, beaten with
   1 tsp corn oil

Preheat oven to 400°F
Grease or paper line muffin pan.

1 *In large bowl, combine all the dry ingredients. Mix well.*
2 *In medium bowl, combine all wet ingredients. Mix well.*
3 *Combine dry and wet ingredients. Stir only to moisten, but batter is lumpy. Spoon into muffin pan and bake 20 to 25 minutes. Remove from pan and cool on rack.*

SERVE THESE MUFFINS FOR A SPECIAL BREAKFAST SURPRISE. THE ALMONDS COMPLETES THE TREAT.

A *CARD-GIFT* Recipe

OAT BRAN *Muffin*

To:

GINGERBREAD

Makes 12 Muffins

DRY INGREDIENTS

1 Cup oat bran
1½ Cups all-purpose flour
1 Tsp baking powder
1 Tsp baking soda
½ Tsp salt
1 Tsp ginger
½ Tsp cinnamon
⅛ Tsp cardomon
3 Tbs brown sugar
1 Tsp non-fat dry milk

WET INGREDIENTS

¼ Cup molasses
¼ Cup margarine, melted
¾ Cup buttermilk
2 Egg whites, beaten with
  1 tsp corn oil
1 Tsp vanilla
½ Cup raisins

*Preheat oven to 400°F
Grease or paper line muffin pan.*

---

1 *In large bowl, combine all the dry ingredients. Mix well.*
2 *In medium bowl, combine all wet ingredients. Mix well.*
3 *Combine dry and wet ingredients. Stir only to moisten, but batter is lumpy. Spoon into muffin pan and bake 20 to 25 minutes. Remove from pan and cool on rack.*

THE FRAGRANCE WILL BRING MEMORIES OF EARLIER YEARS. SERVE PLAIN OR TOP WITH LEMON SAUCE.

A *CARD-GIFT* Recipe

OAT BRAN *Muffin*

To:

RASPBERRY
Makes 12 Muffins

DRY INGREDIENTS

1 Cup oat bran
1¼ Cups all-purpose flour
½ Cup sugar
2½ Tsp baking powder
½ Tsp salt
1 Tsp non-fat dry milk
½ Cup toasted almonds, chopped

WET INGREDIENTS

2 Egg whites, beaten with 1 tsp corn oil
⅔ Cup skim milk
¼ Cup margarine, melted
1 Tsp fresh lemon juice
1 Tsp vanilla
½ Cup coconut
1 Cup fresh raspberries

Preheat oven to 400°F
Grease or paper line muffin pan.

---

1 *In large bowl, combine all the dry ingredients. Mix well.*
2 *In medium bowl, combine all wet ingredients. Mix well.*
3 *Combine dry and wet ingredients. Stir only to moisten, but batter is lumpy. Spoon into muffin pan and bake 20 to 25 minutes. Remove from pan and cool on rack.*

BITS OF RASPBERRIES AND COCONUT MAKES THIS A DELIGHTFUL MUFFIN. TOP WITH HONEY IF DESIRED.

A *CARD-GIFT* Recipe

OAT BRAN *Muffin*

To:

ZUCCHINI NUT
Makes 12 Muffins

DRY INGREDIENTS

⅔ Cup oat bran
⅔ Cup all-purpose flour
⅔ Cup whole wheat flour
½ Cup sugar
3 Tsp baking powder
½ Tsp salt
½ Tsp cinnamon
½ Tsp nutmeg
2 Tsp non-fat dry milk
½ Cup chopped walnuts

WET INGREDIENTS

3 Egg whites, beaten with
  1 tsp corn oil
¼ Cup margarine, melted
¾ Cup skim milk
1 Tsp vanilla
½ Cup coconut flakes
1 Cup shredded zucchini

*Preheat oven to 400°F
Grease or paper line muffin pan.*

---

1 *In large bowl, combine all the dry ingredients. Mix well.*
2 *In medium bowl, combine all wet ingredients. Mix well.*
3 *Combine dry and wet ingredients. Stir only to moisten, but batter is lumpy. Spoon into muffin pan and bake 20 to 25 minutes. Remove from pan and cool on rack.*

EVER-POPULAR ZUCCHINI—FROM SOUP TO MUFFINS, ALWAYS A WINNER.

A *CARD-GIFT* Recipe

OAT BRAN *Muffin*

To:

APRICOT NUT

Makes 12 Muffins

DRY INGREDIENTS

⅔ Cup oat bran
⅔ Cup all-purpose flour
⅔ Cup whole wheat flour
3 Tsp baking powder
1 Tsp cinnamon
½ Tsp nutmeg
2 Tsp non-fat dry milk
½ Cup chopped walnuts

WET INGREDIENTS

½ Cup honey
1 Cup skim milk
2 Egg whites, beaten with
   1 tsp corn oil
¼ Cup margarine, melted
1 Tsp vanilla
¾ Cup chopped dried
   apricots

Preheat oven to 400°F
Grease or paper line muffin pan.

1 In large bowl, combine all the dry ingredients. Mix well.

2 In medium bowl, combine all wet ingredients. Mix well.

3 Combine dry and wet ingredients. Stir only to moisten, but batter is lumpy. Spoon into muffin pan and bake 20 to 25 minutes. Remove from pan and cool on rack.

FULL OF NUTS AND TASTY CHUNKS OF DRIED APRICOT.
SERVE THESE WITH PINEAPPLE JUICE.

A *CARD-GIFT* Recipe

OAT BRAN *Muffin*

To:

ORANGE/BERRY

Makes 12 Muffins

DRY INGREDIENTS

1 Cup oat bran
1½ Cups all-purpose flour
2 Tsp baking powder
½ Tsp salt
½ Cup sugar
1 Tsp non-fat dry milk

WET INGREDIENTS

3 Tbs margarine, melted
¾ Cup fresh orange juice
2 Egg whites, beaten with
  1 tsp corn oil
1 Tsp vanilla
1 Tbs grated orange rind
1 Cup fresh cranberries,
  halved

Preheat oven to 400°F
Grease or paper line muffin pan.

---

1 *In large bowl, combine all the dry ingredients. Mix well.*
2 *In medium bowl, combine all wet ingredients. Mix well.*
3 *Combine dry and wet ingredients. Stir only to moisten, but batter is lumpy. Spoon into muffin pan and bake 20 to 25 minutes. Remove from pan and cool on rack.*

THE AROMA OF THIS MUFFIN WILL FILL THE KITCHEN.
SERVE WARM WITH ORANGE MARMALADE.

A *CARD-GIFT* Recipe

OAT BRAN *Muffin*

To:

NOTES

This book is dedicated to John.
Thank you for being my test taster
for all the different muffins!